Original title:
Fern Fantasies

Copyright © 2025 Creative Arts Management OÜ
All rights reserved.

Author: Eleanor Prescott
ISBN HARDBACK: 978-1-80581-870-0
ISBN PAPERBACK: 978-1-80581-397-2
ISBN EBOOK: 978-1-80581-870-0

Moonlit Fern Fragments

In the glow of the night, ferns dance with glee,
Mice in tuxedos host a wild jamboree.
Crickets strum tunes on leaves so green,
While owls wear spectacles, quite the scene.

Beneath the moon's grin, the shadows prance,
Frogs in top hats leap in a daring dance.
The stars are giggling, twinkling bright,
In this leafy kingdom, all feels just right.

Tales of the Leafy Sanctuary

Once a tree claimed it could sing quite well,
But all it could do was cough and yell.
Squirrels wore bows, quite dapper and spry,
While the raccoons debated who'd bake the pie.

In the hush of the woods, laughter would rise,
As hedgehogs debated the best pizza pies.
A ladybug's laugh could cure any gloom,
In this leafy haven, joy made none fume.

Shades of Nature's Soliloquy

A cactus tried to join the leafy fun,
But its prickly jokes left everyone done.
The lilies rolled eyes at the weeds' bad puns,
While daisies promised to bring the buns.

Rabbits in coats planned a grand feast,
While snails were slow, but they were the least.
Butterflies debated the best hairstyle,
In the wild of whispers, they chatted awhile.

Whispers Among the Wild

Under a canopy, secrets were shared,
Foxes in pajamas, oh how they dared.
Owls told tall tales of the night they flew,
While ants pulled a prank on a beetle or two.

The moss giggled softly as shadows wobbled,
While raccoons enjoyed the snacks they gobbled.
In a world where whimsy pairs with the trees,
Nature chuckles under the breeze.

Beneath the Understory

   In the shade of leaves so wide,
Squirrels gossip, hearts full of pride.
Frogs wear hats, so dapper and spry,
   Joking with beetles that flutter by.

Mushrooms sing with voices so low,
Tickling the toes of the dancing doe.
Raccoons juggling acorns with flair,
While earthworms giggle, light as air.

Sylvan Serenades

In the woods where shadows play,
Chipmunks serenade the day.
Owls hoot in a silly tune,
As dandelions dance with the moon.

Foliage sways like a wild ballerina,
Bugs trading gossip like a hyena.
Bees wear goggles, think they can fly,
While ants organize a conga line nearby.

Dances Among the Moss

Mossy carpets soft and lush,
Caterpillars start to rush.
A party's brewing, join the fun,
While sleepy bears dream of sun.

Worms take turns in a limbo game,
The mushrooms cheer, forgetting their fame.
Fireflies twinkle like stars on the ground,
In this wild waltz of the underground.

Spirit of the Verdant Realm

In a realm where laughter flows,
Funky ferns wear polka-dots nose.
Wily weeds spin tales so tall,
While lazy snakes take the fall.

Merry critters rush to parade,
Gathering stories that never fade.
In this jungle full of delight,
Every shadow holds a giggling light.

Shadows Among the Lush

In a jungle thick, where shadows lurk,
The bushes giggle, oh what a quirk!
A squirrel in tights, prancing so proud,
While a bird in a bow tie sings out loud.

The leaves whisper secrets, oh what a chat,
As ants in a line wear a tiny hat!
A raccoon juggles with fruits on a spree,
In this wild comedy, all nature's free!

The Mystique of Verdant Dreams

Beneath the loopy vines and bright hues,
A frog sings high notes in its best shoes.
The daisies all waltz, twirling with glee,
In a dance-off with bees, oh what a spree!

A rabbit dons glasses, reads tales of old,
While caterpillars trade their marigold.
With laughter like bubbles, they pop and they fizz,
In these silly moments, we truly live!

Unraveled Tales of Verdure

In a patch of green, where the mischief flows,
A hedgehog types tales with quill and prose.
With mushrooms as seats, they gather around,
To hear wild adventures, oh what a sound!

The fireflies giggle, lighting the stage,
As a snail in a tuxedo takes center page.
With rambunctious laughter, they weave a great plot,
In a world where the frivolous is all that they've got!

The Lattice of Nature's Lore

In leafy abyss, where laughter is spun,
The vines form a maze, a jungle of fun.
A fox in a monocle reads from a book,
As butterflies dance with each playful crook.

Caterpillars munch on sweet candy canes,
While lizards in sunglasses bask in the lanes.
Underneath the tall trees, they gather in flocks,
Telling tall tales while wearing fine frocks!

The Glimpse of the Woodland Fae

In the shadow of the trees, they play,
Little sprites, in the light of day.
With tiny wings that flutter and twist,
They dance and giggle, a whimsical mist.

One tripped on a root, oh what a sight!
Tangled in grass, in pure delight.
With laughter ringing through the glade,
They're hiding treasures, effortlessly laid.

A mushroom hat worn, so silly and round,
They prance around without making a sound.
A toadstool throne where they sip on dew,
And pull silly faces, oh, who knew?

In a twinkling moment, they vanish with glee,
Leaving behind only whispers of spree.
Next time you're lost in the woods so grand,
Look for the laughter, don't miss their band!

Whispers of the Leaf

The leaves chat loudly, a bustling buzz,
They cackle and chuckle, just because.
A squirrel nearby rolls his eyes in jest,
Complaining of acorns, he's had quite the fest.

One leaf took a dive, oh what a thrill,
Surveying the ground for a soft, gentle spill.
It landed on grass, and the others all cheered,
A leaf on the ground? Yes, that's what we feared!

There's gossip aplenty among branches tall,
About the pine's poker face—so serious, after all.
But when the wind blows, they shake and they sway,
In a tangle of stories, they laugh and display.

Then comes the rain, a ticklish surprise,
The leaves shriek in joy, dancing with cries.
With puddles below, the fun's just begun,
Splashes of laughter, oh, look how they run!

Enchanted Canopy Dreams

Under the branches, a curious sight,
The shadows are shifting from day into night.
A raccoon in pajamas, so utterly spry,
Playing hide and seek, oh me, oh my!

With twinkling stars as the curtain's reveal,
They chat about nuts and the best way to steal.
A firefly wiggles, so bright in its flight,
Lighting the jokes that echo at night.

A hedgehog rolls by, full of grumbles and sighs,
"Why do they call me cute? What a pack of lies!"
Yet joined in the fun, with a chuckle or two,
Wiggling his spines, he's ready to brew.

The laughter and joy around sprinkle so bright,
They dream of tomorrows full of delight.
In a world full of wonder, let the forest scheme,
Where everything's giggles and all is a dream!

The Lilt of Fronds

In a garden where the fronds do dance,
Lively bogeymen invite a prance.
Silly spirits swirl around the leaves,
Bouncing with the laughs that nature weaves.

A wiggle here, a shuffle there,
Who knew green could hold such flair?
Funky fungi join in with glee,
Underneath the shade of the leafy spree.

Marshmallow bunnies hop in the shade,
Chasing after light and lemonade.
Tiny toadstools giggle and sway,
In this party of green, come what may.

So come now, friends, let's raise a cheer,
For leafy tomfoolery that brings us near.
With the sun high above, let's play along,
In the jolly green world where we belong!

Wildwood Murmurs

In the thick of woods where whispers play,
Squirrels hold council about the day.
They chuckle and chatter, oh what a sight,
Telling tall tales until the night.

Mice don spectacles, recite their prose,
While hedgehogs hum tunes only they know.
A raccoon shows dance moves, all very sly,
With twirls that could make the moon go shy.

The trees lean closer to hear the fun,
As every bush joins in under the sun.
Even the brook sings a bubbly tune,
Celebrating mischief 'neath the warm afternoon.

So let's not be shy, let's join the show,
With jigs and laughs, let the wildwoods glow.
For in the whispers where mysteries dwell,
Lies the humor of the forest, where all is well!

Emerald Enchantment

Beneath the canopy, secrets unfold,
Where the mossy floor is bright and bold.
Entertaining elves skip on their toes,
With laughter ringing where the wildwind blows.

A gnome in a hat, too large for his head,
Tells jokes to the flowers, they giggle instead.
Tickled by sunbeams, daisies take flight,
Waltzing together till the fall of night.

Glistening dew drips like beads of joy,
While a caterpillar plots like a sly little boy.
The orchids discuss the latest in style,
Compliments flying, mile after mile.

So stop and take heed while wandering through,
For emerald magic brings life anew.
In this forest of folly, find your delight,
As we dance in the shadows, from morning 'til night!

Whimsical Understory

In the depths of the green, a party unfolds,
Where mushrooms in jackets share stories untold.
A rabbit with glasses reads aloud,
While giggling fairies form a curious crowd.

Beetles in tuxedos, doing the twist,
Who knew they'd be experts in the art of bliss?
Crickets recite their bedtime rhymes,
As the dappled light dances in endless climbs.

A snail with a monocle walks the fine line,
Debating the merits of tea and wine.
Under leaves of grandeur, a bash is set,
Where laughter and joy are the best duet.

Join this merry gathering, lively and bright,
In the magical shadows where laughter takes flight.
For in the underbrush, oh what a spree,
Comedic wonders await for you and me!

Sighs of the Leafy Enclave

In a grove where laughter grows,
Leaves play tricks and tease their foes.
The squirrels giggle, dance around,
While mushrooms wobble on the ground.

Chirping birds join in the jest,
Their melodies, a cheeky quest.
A snail slips by with a quirky grin,
Claiming he's the fastest in the din.

Sunlight filters through the shade,
Casting shadows, a grand parade.
A rabbit trips on a grassblade's tip,
And all the critters start to quip.

So if you wander where the fun is,
Join the creatures, catch their fizz!
In the enclave where all is bright,
Laughter echoes day and night.

Dappled Dreams

Beneath the boughs where shadows play,
Frogs in hats croak 'hip-hip-hooray!'
Dancing fireflies twirl with glee,
While ants throw a wild jubilee.

A chipmunk juggles acorns tall,
Claiming he's the best of all.
A wheezy owl can't help but cheer,
As nearby bunnies slice up beer.

The grass grows tall, but who can care?
With all this fun, why would we dare?
To worry 'bout the world outside,
When nature's chorus is our guide!

So let the whimsies bring delight,
In dappled dreams that last through night.
With every rustle, every sound,
Joy emerges from the ground.

Thickets of Tranquility

In thickets deep where secrets hum,
A lazy lizard starts to drum.
Bees with ties are buzzin' around,
While wise old tortoises are crowned.

A wacky wind plays peek-a-boo,
It tickles leaves, oh what a view!
Caterpillars rolling, no cares at all,
As drowsy bees begin to brawl.

A hedgehog dons a spiky hat,
Claiming he's the king of that!
And all the creatures stop to gawk,
As they gather 'round to have a talk.

In this thicket where silliness reigns,
Laughter echoes through the lanes.
So if you find a twinkling spot,
Join in the fun, don't miss the lot!

Whirling in the Green Abyss

In the valleys, fun spins 'round,
With dandelions dancing on the ground.
A laughing brook joins in the fray,
Telling stories in a playful way.

A chipmunk chases bubbles in the air,
While squirrels plot without a care.
The sun, a jester, paints the sky,
As clouds wear silly hats up high.

A party of worms wiggle to the beat,
While shadows sway on silly feet.
The daisies giggle, roots entwined,
Whirling in a pas de deux, so unconfined.

When twilight hushes every sound,
The whispers of joy swirl all around.
In the green abyss, let laughter flow,
For in this realm, all joy must grow.

Cascading Greenery

In a forest where ferns pirouette,
Lizards in bow ties groove, don't forget.
Squirrels trade nuts for dance cards, oh my!
Mushrooms throw parties, just pass on the pie.

Leaves whisper secrets, with giggles so light,
Frogs wear top hats, preparing for flight.
A breeze brings laughter, tickles the air,
Even the old oak shakes off despair.

Beetles in tuxedos roll out the plan,
To shine at the ball, they all take a stand.
Dancing and prancing, a critter parade,
No one can stop them; they just can't be swayed.

Under the twilight, the green turns to gold,
With all those grand moves, the stories unfold.
In this wild comedy, who would have guessed,
That ferns are the stars at this woodland fest?

Intricate Patterns of Life

In the underbrush, the patterns collide,
Gnomes knit the threads where the fairies abide.
A spider named Larry gives fashion advice,
Tells grasshoppers, "Sparkle, it's quite precise!"

Shadows are dancing in loops and in swirls,
A flock of bugs zooms, adding glitz to their twirls.
Worms in sunglasses lounge under the sun,
Chasing their tails, oh, isn't this fun?

Flowers wear hats from the brightly-hued field,
While ants host a rave, their secrets revealed.
The daisies do breakdancing, splendid and spry,
As dragonflies spin like they own the blue sky.

Nature's a circus—come laugh and admire,
Even the roots have a dance to inspire.
In this quilt of life, where chaos can reign,
We find the most joy in the sweet silly strain.

Sylva's Soft Sighs

With a rustle and hush, Sylva gives way,
To whispers of dreams that dart and sway.
A rabbit in sneakers gets ready to hop,
While a turtle named Timmy just won't stop.

Gladiolus stand proud in their pastel attire,
They giggle at squirrels who play with a wire.
Branches are grinning, their leaves in a tease,
As chipmunks compose songs—oh, if you please!

Mushrooms in minstrels, perform at the glade,
Playing their beats in a mossy upgrade.
The sound of soft laughter spreads through the wood,
Where the joy of the forest is perfectly good.

Under this canopy, fun knows no bounds,
Even the raindrops compose goofy sounds.
Sylva keeps sighing, with happiness brimming,
In her embrace, life feels light and bright, glimmering.

Dreamweaver's Woodland

In Dreamweaver's realm, under starlit trails,
Fairies bake cookies while telling tall tales.
Rabbits in capes dance about with delight,
While owls wear spectacles for a clearer sight.

Nimble and swift, the fireflies dart,
Painting the night with art from the heart.
A hedgehog in socks surveys with a grin,
As the moon starts to giggle, it beckons them in.

Pinecones are treasures; squirrels hold them dear,
Trading them for secrets, the latest gossip here.
The trees sway in rhythm to the woodland's beat,
While the roots banter softly, no one skips a beat.

At dawn, the cloak of night fades away,
With stories and laughter to cherish each day.
In Dreamweaver's Woodland, where all are so spry,
The fun never falters, and spirits soar high.

The Dreamweaver's Grove

In a grove where giggles grow,
Trees wear hats of leafy glow.
Squirrels dance with acorn crowns,
While mushrooms play and twirl around.

A rabbit juggles carrots high,
As birds in suits take to the sky.
The sunlight beams, a golden chime,
In this place, it's always prime.

A fox in socks, quite out of place,
Tripped on vines, fell with grace.
Laughter echoes, soft and sweet,
In this grove, it's hard to beat.

So join the fun, toss worries away,
There's always room for more to play.
With every twist and every turn,
In the grove, we all can learn.

Spirals of Green Wonder

Spin in circles, let out a cheer,
In patches green, there's fun right here.
Dancing leaves on a breezy day,
Whispering secrets in a play.

A snail in glasses reading a book,
Tipsy mushrooms, oh, take a look!
Worms in ties hold a debate,
Over who should be the next great mate.

Laughter rolls like the clouds above,
Nature's gifts, a life to love.
In spirals bright, we twist and sway,
In this green realm, we'll always stay.

So raise a toast to the sunlit skies,
Where every critter has a surprise.
From winding paths to the joyful hum,
In green wonder, we always come.

An Odyssey in the Understory

Beneath the boughs, where shadows play,
An odyssey in a funny way.
A hedgehog quests for the biggest snack,
While ants on bikes zoom down the track.

A lizard in a cape, oh so bold,
Claims the title of the bravest gold.
While beetles race in tiny cars,
Dreaming of being the next big stars.

In nooks and crannies, giggles burst,
With tiny flowers that always thirst.
They sip the dew, oh what a scene,
In this cozy, leafy green routine.

So wander down this merry lane,
Where every step is pure champagne.
In the understory, let's all rejoice,
In nature's wild, we find our voice.

Lush Whispers

In the hush of a leafy glade,
Lush whispers come, not to evade.
A raccoon's wearing pajamas neat,
And shares a laugh with his friends so sweet.

The owls hoot jokes in the night sky,
While crickets chirp with a twinkle in eye.
Frogs in tuxedos sing in tune,
Their croaky ballads make hearts swoon.

A dance-off starts with a vibrant flair,
Two snails in rhythm, quite the affair.
From ferns and fronds, the laughter flies,
In this lush realm, joy never dies.

So tiptoe softly, join in the fun,
In nature's winks, we're never done.
With every rustle and every sway,
In lush whispers, we laugh and play.

The Hidden Grove

In the grove where shadows swing,
Laughter's echo makes hearts sing.
Giggling leaves with secrets bright,
    Dance together in the night.

    A squirrel in a tiny hat,
  Steals acorns like a sneaky brat.
He winks his eye, takes off in glee,
His little kingdom, wild and free.

The tree trunks wear a barky grin,
While playful vines invite folks in.
   A party hosted by the trees,
With drinks that taste like honey bees!

So come and join this leafy spree,
In the hidden grove, just you and me.
We'll twirl and shout, let laughter fly,
  Beneath the stars, in a leafy sky.

Oxygen Dreams

In a world where plants conspire,
Breathing deep with dreams like fire.
Leaves are chatting, not too shy,
Whispering secrets as we pass by.

A cactus dressed in sparkly shoes,
Dances off to shake off blues.
While daisies giggle, planning pranks,
Plotting mischief with leafy flanks.

Dreams of green float on the breeze,
As succulents giggle with such ease.
Petals twirling, what a show,
In a garden, we won't outgrow.

So take a breath and join the fun,
In a world where laughter's spun.
Let the wonders lift your heart,
In this dreamland, play your part.

Beneath the Tropical Veil

Underneath the tropic trees,
Coconuts swing in the playful breeze.
With monkey royalty on parade,
Jokes and jests in the leafy shade.

A parrot joking in bright colors,
Mocks the folks, the party lovers.
"Polly wants a cracker!" it squeals,
While hiding behind an ivy's wheels.

The palm fronds flap like excited hands,
Encouraging joy to fill the lands.
Laughter echoes, a melodic gale,
As we dance beneath this vibrant veil.

So come and dance where wild things play,
In a tropical twist, we'll sway away.
With sun-kissed smiles and sparkling eyes,
We'll weave our dreams beneath the skies.

Moondrenched Foliage

Under moonlight, leaves take flight,
Whispering tales that spark delight.
A raccoon with a marshmallow dream,
Plans a feast with a quirky theme.

Glow-worms twinkle in a line,
As owls hoot with wisdom fine.
Odd critters throw a midnight bash,
With snacks that make the petunias flash.

The grass giggles beneath our feet,
As fireflies dance to a night-time beat.
Conversations of crickets play,
In the moon's embrace, we laugh and sway.

So join the fun in this starlit dance,
Where every moment's a silly chance.
With nature's whimsy all around,
In moondrenched foliage, joy is found.

Secrets Beneath the Fronds

In the shade where whispers play,
Little critters plot all day.
A squirrel dons a tiny hat,
While the owls giggle, 'Isn't that fat?'

Frogs in bow ties leap around,
Singing songs with the plump ground.
Rabbits dance with glee and cheer,
Declaring it the best day of the year!

Snakes slither in and spill the tea,
While the skunks dance quite carefree.
They spin and twirl beneath green leaves,
Creating a ruckus, just to tease!

What secrets hide under the cover?
Engines of laughter that make us hover.
Join the fun, don't be a bore,
There's magic brewing, just explore!

Green Veils of Enchantment

In a garden dressed in shades so bright,
The daisies wink, say, 'What a sight!'
A snail in a race, how absurdly slow,
While the butterflies flaunt their vibrant glow.

Gnomes play cards with mysterious shrooms,
Telling tales that go zoom zoom zoom!
The hedgehogs wear spectacles, oh so chic,
Sharing gossip, quite unique!

Beneath the leaves, the magic stirs,
As fireflies light up in gleeful flurrs.
A bug band plays tunes of mischief,
Creating giggles, life's real gift!

A dance of delight, round and round,
Where every creature's joy is found.
Come join us here, in this fairytale,
Where laughter flows like a warm spring trail!

Dance of the Forest Spirits

In the woods, what a sight to behold,
Where spirits sparkle, forever bold!
They twirl and spin with laughter loud,
Hiding dreams beneath the crowd.

A scruffy raccoon leads the way,
While chipmunks chirp and grandly sway.
Trees clap their hands, big and wide,
As the critters join in for the ride!

When shadows loom and sparkles fall,
The sprites begin their vibrant ball.
With mushrooms as chairs and acorns for drinks,
Wise old owls just chuckle and wink!

Oh, what shenanigans take the stage,
In the deep green woods, let's disengage!
For under the stars, our worries cease,
And laughter reigns, our hearts in peace!

Sylvan Daydreams

Under canopies of dreams so sly,
The trees gossip like passersby.
A rabbit wears shoes, oh so neat,
While foxes giggle at their own feet.

The streams murmur secrets in a rush,
While butterflies lounge without a hush.
Pinecones sport caps of worry-free flair,
Tickling the noses of squirrels in air!

Dancing leaves tumble in a fray,
As the festival of squirrels plays its way.
Songs of the unseen sprinkle light,
In the green embrace, a joyous sight!

With laughter echoing through the trees,
Join the merriment, feel the breeze.
In the world where whimsy finds a home,
Life becomes a joyful poem!

Petals in the Mist

In the garden where squirrels play,
Petals giggle and sway all day.
A caterpillar ordered a pizza,
While a snail raced, but lost to a cheetah.

The daisies danced in their fancy hats,
While butterflies critiqued their acrobat chats.
A bee tried to sing, but it's quite clear,
He was better at buzzing, I'll give it a cheer!

The sun winked at roses in bloom,
As frogs croaked their best tunes of gloom.
But laughter erupted from bees in a line,
Who formed a conga with a touch of fine wine!

So, let's toast to the whimsy that grows,
In gardens where silliness always glows.
For under the petals, a party will start,
With laughter and joy, it's a work of art!

Fern-touched Dreams

In a dreamland where mushrooms wear shoes,
Frogs play hopscotch, singing the blues.
A rabbit in shades sips his tea,
While a hedgehog debates who's the best rapper, hee-hee!

Clouds made of cotton candy float by,
As birds with pajamas giggle and fly.
A skunk in a tutu prances with pride,
While fireflies light up like they're opening wide.

The stars chuckle softly from up above,
Watching the dance of a critter's true love.
But a raccoon slipped on a banana peel,
And the laughter erupted with every squeal!

So close your eyes and join the spree,
In a world where the quirky roam free.
With critters that twirl and a giggle or two,
It's a whimsical night; join the crew!

The Sylvan Beneath

In the woods where oddities bloom,
A squirrel juggles acorns, creating a room.
Foxes play tag with the shadows of trees,
While owls crack jokes that bring them to knees.

A rabbit in slippers sips on fresh dew,
An iguana on stilts moonwalks, it's true!
A deer runs a bakery that sells just one pie,
While woodpeckers tweet as the days hurry by.

The mushrooms hold parties under hot sun,
With pixies and gnomes till the woodwork is done.
A turtle, quite sleepy, takes up the front row,
As the hedgehogs dispute who can giggle the most.

Let's laugh through the leaves and dance on the ground,
For magic and mischief here shall be found.
With creatures galore and a chuckle or cheer,
In this sylvan realm, the fun is quite clear!

Woodland Lullabies

In the woods, where the shadows sway,
A badger hums lullabies at the end of the day.
While crickets chirp in tuxedos and ties,
The fireflies twinkle like miniature skies.

A raccoon croons softly by the old creek,
While the chipmunks clap to the tunes they seek.
Frogs gather round with their tiny green hats,
As the owls roll their eyes, saying, "Not this, chaps!"

With mushrooms that glow in a colorful dance,
The pixies invite each creature to prance.
A bear with a banjo strums to the beat,
While mouse in a dress reveals her best feet.

So close your eyes and sway in your dreams,
To the woodland's music and laughter that beams.
For under the stars, every critter agrees,
The night's just a riot of woodland trapeze!

Tapestries of Earth

In a garden wild, gnome hats fly,
A snail does jazz, oh me, oh my!
The daisies dance, with pirouettes,
While a worm in shades debates life debts.

A wily raccoon steals a pie,
With a wink and a grin, oh my oh my!
He tells a joke, as the ants all cheer,
Saying life's a feast, don't shed a tear.

A hedgehog dons a tutu bright,
Spinning like a disco light.
With each turn, leaves swirl around,
This fancy ball's the talk of town!

So if you hear a giggle near,
It's the woodland folk, let's give a cheer!
They spin their tales in joy and mirth,
In the whimsical tapestries of earth.

Secrets of Sylvan Beckons

Whispers float from twigs and trees,
As squirrels plan their mischievous fees.
A woodpecker raps a snappy beat,
While chipmunks shuffle their tiny feet.

A fox in shoes tries to dance,
But trip he does, no second chance!
He sprawls on leaves with a comical thud,
And swears he'll leave behind the mud.

Beneath bright mushrooms, secrets hide,
Where mushrooms giggle and help you slide.
Goblins play with glittery rocks,
While a sneaky owl shrugs and mocks.

In the sylvan glades, laughter is grand,
As all creatures join the merry band.
So hush now, for the night time beckons,
To stories where joy endlessly reckons.

Under the Dappled Sun

The sun peeks through, a playful tease,
As shadows dance with the rustling leaves.
A ladybug dons shades quite wide,
Sipping nectar by the river's side.

A caterpillar croons a silly song,
While beetles march along in throng.
They twirl and swirl with all their might,
Creating chaos—what a sight!

Bunnies hop in mismatched socks,
While turtles twirl like disco clocks.
The dappled sun, it casts bright fun,
As laughter echoes, one by one.

Under this sky, all worries cease,
As nature sings a tune of peace.
Join in the laughter, come have a run,
For life's a joy, under the sun!

Hidden Trails of Green

In hidden paths, the critters play,
As nature winks, come join the fray.
A squirrel in glasses reads a book,
While frogs in ties give gossip a look.

Mice in ball gowns, ready to twirl,
Make each party a whirl and swirl.
A raccoon magician pulls tricks anew,
With a hat so tall, it's quite the view!

Wandering in these green retreat,
A peacock struts with fashionable feet.
He claims he's the king of the lovely glade,
With each feather bright, a grand charade!

So find your way where the laughter grows,
And let your heart dance, as joy bestows.
In hidden trails where wonders burst,
Come join the fun—oh, you'll be immersed!

Tales from the Forest Floor

In a glade where shadows dwell,
The mushrooms share a joke to tell.
A squirrel giggles, laughs out loud,
While dancing under acorn shroud.

A hedgehog joins with wiggly grace,
Twirling 'round, it's quite a race.
A snail, bemused, keeps up the pace,
While beetles cheer from their safe space.

The trees then whisper, soft and spry,
About a raccoon in a tie.
He trips on roots, a clumsy sight,
And all the woodland bursts with light!

So come and laugh where critters dwell,
In Woodland Tales, they cast their spell.
With punchlines hidden 'neath the leaves,
In every corner, joy retrieves.

Caress of the Thyme

Upon a bed of fragrant thyme,
The ladybugs all sing in rhyme.
With little hats and shoes of lace,
They tap their feet in joyous space.

A frog in boots, he leaps with flair,
While ants parade without a care.
They march to tunes of bubbling brooks,
As caterpillars read their books.

The bees are buzzing quite a tune,
As flowers sway beneath the moon.
With honey jokes that tickle the air,
Each petal grins, their joy to share.

So join the dance of fragrant glee,
Where thyme adores each buzzing bee.
In laughter's grasp, the garden gleams,
In every scent, a world that dreams.

Under the Light Filter

The sunbeams filter through the leaves,
And play with shadows, weave and tease.
A chipmunk peeks with mischief bright,
While butterflies have morning flight.

The old tree stump holds a debate,
While crickets chirp and contemplate.
Who stole the snacks? The nuts, they say!
Was it the owl? Or hedgehog's play?

A lizard wears a tiny hat,
Complaining of the chill—how fat!
He sunbathes on a rock so wide,
While grinning frogs leap by his side.

Each glance reveals a merry sight,
In glimmers of the dancing light.
With laughter bubbling in the air,
These forest friends, beyond compare!

Green Veils of Wonder

Beneath the canopy of green,
The forest plays a merry scene.
With rabbits donning cloaks so grand,
And shy foxes that take a stand.

The clouds float by, like little boats,
As squirrels juggle acorn coats.
A hedgehog reads a book of jokes,
While giggling softly with the folks.

A band of frogs begins to sing,
Their croaking sounds like springtime's fling.
While dandelions sway and spin,
The dance of weeds invites a grin.

So roam among the secret glades,
Where countless jokes and laughter spades.
In green veils, all the wonders peek,
A forest full of joyful squeaks!

Echoes from the Woodland Depths

In sunlight's dance, leaves come alive,
Little critters with plans to thrive.
A squirrel's nut becomes a balmy prize,
While a snail helms a tiny surprise.

With giggles brushing against the bark,
A rabbit sings, it's quite a lark.
The trees whisper secrets, oh so sly,
While mushrooms grin, passing by.

Rabbits in glasses, debating the stars,
Whilst porcupines ponder life behind bars.
A hedgehog's dance, wobbly and round,
While the wise old owl just rolls on the ground.

In capes made of leaves, they play tricks and pranks,
Creating a world where laughter swanks.
Each shadow a giggle, each breeze a cheer,
Echoes of joy the woodland will hear.

Rhapsody in Green

Amidst swirling ferns, a frog plays the lute,
His music so loud, makes the crickets salute.
With hopping and flopping, he leads a parade,
While clovers uncurl, in green masquerade.

The ants wear top hats on tiny great sprees,
As bees waltz around, sipping sweet memories.
A ladybug conducts with much pomp and flair,
While the beetles applaud, without a care.

A fish in a puddle, wearing a crown,
Sings to the winds, never fret nor frown.
The butterflies flutter, in pajamas of silk,
Drinking the sunshine, like sweetened milk.

A chipmunk brings popcorn for all to share,
As the sun sets low, without a single care.
With giggles abounding, the forest takes flight,
In rhapsody echoed, from morning to night.

Treetop Reveries

Up high in the branches, the owlets convene,
Plotting a heist for the best tangerine.
A woodpecker's drumming becomes a big plan,
While the squirrels conspire, 'lil rascals they can!

With acorns as treasures, they barter and play,
As chipmunks sell tickets for their ballet.
The trees sway with laughter, a gentle caress,
As kittens in hammocks wear tiny red dress.

Clouds pass like sheep, as puffs in the blue,
A dragonfly juggles, just for the crew.
While a raccoon with shades leads a karaoke,
The laughter erupts, oh, how funny to see!

With branches of laughter, they swing to the beat,
In treetop reveries, oh what a feat!
A world filled with giggles, where joy finds its pace,
In this playful haven, each creature's a ace.

The Hidden Glades of Imagination

In glades where dreams bounce and rascals convene,
A bear in pink slippers paints vivid scenes.
With tea made from daisies, they sip and they toast,
To fantasies wild, for they're the most boast!

A turtle in shades plays cards with the fox,
While the hedgehog will judge, in his fancy frocks.
The squirrels perform as a lively band,
Each note is a chuckle, each rhythm well planned.

Beneath the great yonder, where laughter won't cease,
A not-so-small dragon dreams of world peace.
With giggles exploding from flowers around,
Imagination flourishes, merriment found.

In this hidden glade where laughter takes flight,
Each critter involved, bringing pure delight.
With imagination's whispers weaving their fun,
They dance through the day 'til the evening is done.

Emerald Dreams woven in Light

In the garden, a lizard prances,
Chasing shadows, taking chances.
A snail in shades of gleeful green,
Sprints for success - if only seen!

Twirling leaves begin to dance,
Tickling toes, it's quite a chance.
A bug plays tunes with tiny drums,
While nearby, the broccoli hums.

Each petal shimmers in the sun,
A sunbeam whispers, 'Let's have fun!'
Colors pop in a joyful race,
Nature's jesters in a vast space.

So leap and skip in leafy paths,
Join the jesters, share the laughs.
With whispers of a breezy jest,
In emerald dreams, let's be our best.

Solstice in Green

On the solstice, frogs wear crowns,
Jumping high, they never frown.
Rippling ponds with glares of wit,
A turtle's dance? It's quite a hit!

Butterflies sport a dazzling show,
Flapping tales of long ago.
A rock who thinks it's quite the star,
Winks at clouds that drift afar.

Napping ants dream in a pile,
Planning parties with great style.
While crickets laugh with tiny breaths,
Inventing new games with no regrets.

Let's toast to leaves and stems anew,
With sips of dew and frothy brew.
Under skies of vibrant hue,
We dance in green - oh what a view!

Reverie of Leafy Labyrinths

In a maze of green, I lost my shoe,
A raccoon laughs - 'What's wrong with you?'
A squirrel plays tag with the swaying vines,
While mushrooms giggle at curious designs.

A wise old oak begins to muse,
'Let's make faces; it's up to you to choose!'
Ferns don hats made of sunbeam rays,
While shadows plot in peculiar ways.

Grape vines climb to steal the show,
Whispering secrets only they know.
The air is thick with giggles and cheers,
As daisies recall their colorful peers.

With twinkling lights and raucous glee,
Join the frolic; it's wild and free.
In leafy lanes where laughter thrives,
The sweetest joy is where fun thrives!

Shimmering Shadows of Nature

Underneath the wide, bright sun,
Shadows giggle, just for fun.
A wise old tree jests, 'Take your seat,'
While creatures gather to feel the beat.

In the glen, a caterpillar spins,
Telling tales of missed win-skins.
A rabbit in shades of bright maroon,
Sings a tune that ends too soon.

Froggy jokes make the pond capsize,
As the dragonfly rolls his eyes.
With a wink, the daisies bloom,
Creating a ruckus, eating up room.

So laugh with me beneath the trees,
Join this revel, let's feel the breeze.
In shimmering shadows, we create,
Stories told by all who relate.

Realm of the Tea-colored Shadows

In the shade where giggles grow,
Mice wear hats, and owls sing low.
Butterflies dance with a jittery flair,
While squirrels sip tea without a care.

The shadows tease with playful tricks,
Jellybeans spill from shadowy brinks.
A dragonfly juggles fireflies bright,
Underneath the lantern light.

A frog in a tuxedo croaks a tune,
Beneath the glow of a clumsy moon.
All the critters join in a waltz,
For laughter, dear friend, never halts.

In this realm of sways and shimmers,
Wonders abound, and joy glimmers.
Every twist reveals a chuckle,
In this land where secrets snuggle.

Nature's Intricate Tapestry

In the woods where the laughter twines,
Chipmunks wear their tiny designs.
One wears plaid, another has stripes,
While ferns giggle and whisper types.

The rabbits knit with twigs and grass,
Creating hats for every pass.
Squirrels spin yarn from soft, warm fluff,
Telling tales of when things get tough.

The trees sway in giggly lines,
Tickling the tales of ancient vines.
Each leaf nods with a playful wink,
As clouds pause to share a drink.

Here in this grid of glee unfurls,
It's a tapestry woven of joy and twirls.
With every thread, a punchline weaves
And the earth chuckles as it breathes.

Lush Labyrinths of Thought

In mazes lush with giggling greens,
Mice play hide and seek in the scenes.
Each turn brings a ticklish surprise,
With laughter echoing 'neath the skies.

An ant in boots prances with glee,
Singing songs of honey and tea.
While rabbits hop on pogo sticks,
In a cirque of silly little tricks.

Thoughts meander like a playful breeze,
Carrying antics through the trees.
A thinking cap made of dandelions,
Bestows witticisms like stand-up lions.

So wander deep, let your mind play,
In these lush fields, let humor sway.
The labyrinths twist with a chuckling sound,
Where clever companions are always found.

Peeking through the Bracken

Beneath green curtains, mischief brews,
Kittens prance in fuzzy shoes.
A lizard with glasses reads a book,
While a turtle plays hide-and-seek by the nook.

Peering through the leafy fray,
Havoc reigns in a playful way.
An owl with a mustache shouts, "hooray!"
As bees wear crowns and lead the ballet.

Frogs are chefs with their jokes on full,
Whipping up soup in a tiny bowl.
Each bubble bursts with raucous cheer,
Echoing laughter that draws us near.

So peek through bracken, let spirits rise,
In this silly world, joy never dies.
With each glance, more mischief to unwind,
The fun awaits, eager and kind.

The Whispering Green

In the garden where giggles grow,
Leaves exchange secrets, don't you know?
A plant with a joke, right out of the blue,
Said, "I'm rooting for you!" with a sprout and a coo.

Sunlight tickles the emerald skirts,
As flowers gossip, sharing their quirks.
A snail slips by with its shell of bad puns,
Winking at bees as they bask in the sun.

A breeze whispers tales of a clumsy old gnome,
Who tried to dance but instead found a home.
With twirls and with swirls, he toppled with flair,
And the daisies all laughed, saying, "That's quite a scare!"

So come take a peek where the silly leaves play,
Join in their laughter, don't shy away!
Nature's a stage for the weird and the bright,
Where even the grass grins from morning till night.

Overgrowth Odyssey

In a jungle of weeds, where the chaos reigns,
Laughter erupts as the garden entertains.
A tomato in spectacles, fretting its size,
Said, "I'm feeling saucy!" with bright, twinkling eyes.

Vines twist and giggle, a wriggly dance,
As carrots do somersaults, taking a chance.
A cucumber juggles with ease and with flair,
While peppers are planning their next comedy dare.

A mushroom spins tales as the sun starts to set,
Of sprites that get tangled in a green minuet.
In the land of the wild, where the laughter is bold,
Even weeds weave stories that never grow old.

So join the expedition, leave worries behind,
For nature's a party where silliness binds.
The thickets and thorns simply can't hide,
The chuckles and giggles that swirl side by side.

Fables of the Foliage

Beneath the big oak, the shadows conspire,
With critters and whispers, plotting their lyre.
A wise old tree tells of a squirrel's leap,
That ended with acorns! Oh, laughs piled in heaps.

The daisies all chime in with their own silly tale,
Of a worm who thought he could put on a veil.
He married a flower, but the wind made a fuss,
And it blew him away with a giggle and gust!

A lizard rehearses, a stand-up set strong,
He quips about flies—"They don't last so long!"
While ladybugs chuckle, they're rolling in dew,
With wings waving wildly, enjoying the view.

So gather around and hear nature's jest,
Where foliage fables are surely the best.
In the laughter of leaves, you'll find a great treasure,
For humor and green are a natural pleasure.

Moss-covered Mysteries

In a glen thick with moss, secrets hide in the folds,
A toad gives a wink, with a story retold.
His croaks carry meaning, with each tiny blip,
"Life's a big hop, just enjoy every trip!"

The shadows do chuckle as ferns flap their fronds,
While mushrooms are giggling in fun little bonds.
They gathered around with a tea party flair,
Sipping on dewdrops, with laughter to spare.

A hedgehog, a bard, with a quill made of thorn,
Sings songs of the grass that are silly and worn.
"Why did the leaf fall? Just to make way for fun!"
As snickers ring out in the soft morning sun.

So wander and whisper through thickets of cheer,
Where humor and moss weave stories so dear.
Each rustle a chuckle, each petal a grin,
In this quirky green world, let the laughter begin!

Beneath the Canopy: A Reverie

In the shade, where shadows play,
A squirrel schemes his leafy day.
With acorns lined like jewels of gold,
He plans his heist, brave and bold.

A chatty bird with a beak so bright,
Mocks the rabbit, who hops with fright.
"I've stolen seeds from Mr. Hare!"
The forest giggles, without a care.

Luscious vines twist, a jester's hat,
The wise old owl just rolls his mat.
"Join the party or lose your crown!"
Says the fox with a paper gown.

Laughter echoes through tree and bush,
In this green world, there's never a rush.
With every rustle, the fun ignites,
Under the canopy, pure delight bites.

Whimsy in the Underbrush

A beetle dons a tiny tie,
While butterflies just zoom on by.
"Let's throw a bash under this leaf!"
Cried the ant, who's quite the chief.

The snails line up for the slow dance,
To sway beneath the raindrop's prance.
"You'll never find a better floor!"
Shouted the worm, who then did soar.

Raccoons gather for a midnight feast,
With crunchy snacks, at least not least.
"Pepper's chili? What a dare!"
Chortled the owl with a feathered flair.

In this tangle of giggles and glee,
The forest winks as spirits agree.
Crafting fun as the moonlight glows,
In the underbrush, anything goes!

The Alchemy of Leafy Dreams

A magician mouse with a wand of grass,
Turns clovers into treats that people pass.
"Tabby, my friend, come take your share!"
He giggled and tossed with a flair.

Dancing mushrooms stunned with surprise,
As toads in tuxes began to rise.
"A gala tonight? You jest, you fool!"
Chortled a bug, who skipped school.

Petals dive like a jester's prank,
A parade of scents, a fragrant tank.
Caterpillars joke, and ladybugs cheer,
As the forest erupts, so crystal clear.

With laughter blooming through leafy seams,
Life's alchemy flares with magic dreams.
Beneath the twigs, where joys align,
A realm of whimsy, simply divine.

Secrets Among the Brambles

Among the thorns, a secret lies,
A chubby hedgehog with curious eyes.
"I've spotted treasures, all around!"
He whispered low, without a sound.

The rabbits plot with a chuckle and hop,
To steal the best from the berry top.
"Let's ripe the fruit before it's gone!"
Winked the mischief, just at dawn.

A cautious badger with a giggling grin,
Tripped over roots, and launched a spin.
"Who turned this path into a maze?"
He grumbled, lost in a bind of praise.

Secrets wrap like a blanket snug,
While the bramble holds a playful tug.
In every bush, where laughter's found,
There's always magic lurking around.

The Florist's Daydream

In a shop where blooms do dance,
Colors clash, they take a chance.
Roses gossip, lilies laugh,
A daisy's joke is quite the gaffe.

Petals prance on airy breeze,
Tulips tease, they do as they please.
Sunflowers strike a silly pose,
Carnations giggle, everyone knows.

Vases full of floral cheer,
Plants plotting mischief, never fear.
A tulip whispers, 'Look at me!'
'I'm the star, can't you see?'

With each stem, a tale unfolds,
Botanical pranks, daring and bold.
Oh, the fun within these walls,
Where nature's humor gladly calls.

Curves of Nature's Charm

In the garden, vines entwine,
Looping round on purpose, fine.
One sprout boasts a twisty trick,
While another's play is quite the kick.

Bending, swaying, grass does dance,
In the sunlight, grasses prance.
A flower giggles, sways in fun,
Shaking petals under the sun.

The trees are plotting silly games,
Whispering wind adds to their claims.
Branches bow like haughty kings,
While the daisies burst with springs.

Nature's quirks are pure delight,
Creating laughter, day and night.
With each curve and clever bend,
A joyous tale, it seems, won't end.

Lingering in the Leafy Abode

In a nook where shadows hide,
Leaves unfold, their laughter wide.
Caterpillars play a prank,
While squirrels put on a show, no blank.

Mushrooms giggle, spreading cheer,
Telling stories that we hear.
With each rustle, whispers rise,
Nature's secrets, oh, what a surprise!

Breezes carry funny tales,
Riding on the wind that sails.
Crowning ferns with leafy crowns,
As laughter echoes, round the towns.

In leafy homes, fun abounds,
With each rustle, joy surrounds.
As shades and sounds keep filling the air,
A whimsical world beyond compare.

Sylvan Secrets

In the woods where shadows play,
Trees conspire, come what may.
An acorn tosses out a dare,
'Bet you can't catch me in mid-air!'

Moss giggles, soft and green,
'You've never seen my sneaky scene!'
With every sway, the branches tease,
Squirrels fumble, oh what a breeze!

Beneath the ferns, a party brews,
Gnomes debate what joke to choose.
With raccoons serving prized cheese,
A feast of fun that aims to please.

Sylvan life is pure delight,
Where secrets laugh in day and night.
With whispers in the leaves above,
Nature dances in a world of love.

Ferns in Moonlit Reverie

In the night's soft glow, they sway,
Whispering secrets in a playful way.
With a giggle, they dance in a trance,
Under the moon, they start to prance.

Tiny hats on leafy heads,
Playing tag among the beds.
They tickle toes that wander near,
With every rustle, laughter's here.

A critter peers from under leaf,
Joining dance, their silent chief.
Full of glee, they spin and twirl,
In this moonlit swirl, oh what a whirl!

And when the dawn paints skies anew,
They yawn and stretch, begin to strew.
With fuzzy fronds, they bid good night,
Waiting for fun in the next moonlight.

Nature's Hidden Whimsy

A patch of green with a cheeky grin,
Surprises hide where laughter's been.
They poke and prod with leaves so sly,
Making mischief as the days go by.

Who knew a plant could tell a joke?
With twirls and spins, they're never broke.
Rolling on the ground, oh what a sight!
Their humor shines in the warm sunlight.

There's one with curls that tickle toes,
While another winks where the breeze blows.
Nature's clowns on a stage so grand,
With humor crafted by a gentle hand.

As shadows stretch and evening calls,
They skedaddle, twirling, doing sprawls.
Left behind is their giggly trace,
In the garden, they'll always embrace.

The Ballet of Green Tendrils

A troupe of greens takes center stage,
In a cosmic dance, they engage.
With pirouettes and leaps of joy,
Each leaf a dancer, each frond a toy.

Frogs leap in with a cheer so loud,
Joining in, they feel so proud.
The ferns twirl, the critters clap,
In this whimsical, leafy lap.

With a flutter here and a sway so bold,
Their story of laughter and fun unfolds.
In this ballet, no rules apply,
What matters most is to laugh and fly.

As twilight falls, the dance gives way,
To sleepy thoughts at the end of play.
And with a bow, they bid farewell,
To share more tales, their magic to tell.

Ethereal Growths

Up and down, they jiggle and shake,
As if the earth itself had its wake.
Tiny whispers float on air,
Each curl and twist, a story to share.

Beneath the sun, they play hide and seek,
Little green gnomes, so cheeky and meek.
They bubble with laughter, making a fuss,
As they blend in with the dandelion bus.

In a breeze, they're statuesque,
Yet funny faces emerge, grotesque.
With moonlit giggles, secrets unfurl,
A waltz with shadows in a twirling whirl.

At dusk, they huddle, snug and tight,
Planning stunts for the next night.
So here's the tale of plants that play,
Ethereal jesters in nature's display.

The Caress of Nature

In the garden, plants wear hats,
Twirling in the breeze like acrobats.
Silly daisies dance with flair,
While cactus pricks the unaware.

Butterflies wear polka dots,
Chasing shadows, tying knots.
Laughter echoes through the leaves,
As nature's jester quietly weaves.

Frogs leap high on lily pads,
Each landing makes the water glad.
A squirrel tries to steal a snack,
And loses in a comical whack.

The sun, a giant disco ball,
Spins light upon the garden hall.
While gnomes in suits play charades,
In a world where whimsy invades.

Sylvan Delights

The trees boast faces, funny grins,
Tickling leaves like playful twins.
Owls wear spectacles, reading books,
While rabbits in coats share funny looks.

A chorus of crickets sings a tune,
Under the watchful eye of the moon.
Raccoons raid trash cans for a treat,
In a scavenger hunt on tiny feet.

Mushrooms giggle, pop up with glee,
"I'm more colorful!" says the fungi spree.
Squirrels trade secrets in high tree nooks,
Plotting mischief with silly hook looks.

The sun slips down, the stars take stage,
Fireflies dance, the night's own page.
With laughter wrapped in evening's cloak,
Nature's jesters make the world bespoke.

Dimensions of Greenery

In a land where greens leap high,
Veils of vines waltz and sigh.
Pants wear stripes, flowers sing,
Apple trees play the king.

Birds crack jokes on tangled vines,
Chattering about dinner lines.
A rabbit sports a floppy hat,
Pretending to be something fat.

Lettuce plays tag with the corn,
While garlic thinks it's newly born.
Pumpkins tell tales of Halloween,
Making laughter widely seen.

Sunflowers nod with silly grace,
Swapping stories in their space.
In this world of green delight,
The moon becomes a laughing sight.

Emerald Wings at Twilight

In twilight's glow, the bugs unite,
With sparkles and giggles that ignite.
Dragonflies waltz in a daze,
While one takes a slide down a sunbeam's phase.

Moths in capes perform their shows,
Flapping around with flair that glows.
A cricket composes, lost in thought,
Creating melodies in the spots he sought.

Worms in bow ties spin their dance,
Enticing ants with a charming glance.
The fireflies light up the stage,
With sparkling hats they start to engage.

As night unfolds, it's clear to see,
Nature's laughter sets spirits free.
In emerald wings and delusional sighs,
The twilight's magic fills the skies.

Tales from the Green Underbelly

In the garden, gnomes conspire,
With twinkles and laughter, they never tire.
A snail is a knight, a worm is a squire,
They plot on lettuce, their leafy empire.

A cabbage offers a throne of leaves,
Where beetles toast with veggie beve's.
In this kingdom, all are thieves,
Stealing bites from lunch whilst one grieves.

A butterfly rolls in a dance so spry,
While ladybugs teach a wiggly lie.
"Who says we can't eat a slice of sky?"
They giggle and flutter, oh my, oh my!

In shadows of mushrooms, secrets sprout,
Old toadstools gossip while crickets shout.
In this underbelly, there's no doubt,
Laughter grows wild, and joy's about.

The Magic of Swaying Shadows

In the twilight, shadows dance bright,
Pants too big for a toad's delight.
A flower's giggle, a silly sight,
As whispers of magic take flight.

A breezy gust sends leaves on a chase,
Grasshoppers prance in a comical race.
With each little hop, they find their place,
In the wild world of this grassy space.

A frond waves hello, and what's that cheer?
A sheepish squirrel, too bold for fear!
He spins in circles, giving a sneer,
While owls roll their eyes, "Oh dear, oh dear!"

The night is alive with giggles galore,
Under starlit skies, they call for more.
In this magic, we find folklore,
Where shadows sway, and spirits soar.

Veins of Life: A Green Tapestry

A vine starts a brawl with a sneaky fern,
Claiming the sun, oh when will they learn?
In a leafy debate, both twist and turn,
While petals applaud, "When will you burn?"

The roots start a rumor, the soil's ablaze,
With worms giving comments, oh what a phase!
They laugh over snacks like leaves in a daze,
Enjoying the sunshine, lost in a haze.

A creeping moss tells a story so bold,
Of mischief and pranks in the damp and cold.
"Watch out for squirrels with secrets untold,"
They laugh and they cackle, the camaraderie gold.

In the patterns of green, a network does thrive,
Where humor and whimsy keep dreams alive.
The tapestry breathes, and the gags take a dive,
In laughter and life, nature's alive!

Gossamer Dreams of the Glade

In the gloaming, fairies twirl and spin,
With gossamer gowns, they're bound to win.
They tease the moon, "Try joining in!"
While crickets tap dance, with a cheeky grin.

A deer cracks jokes about a moth's flight,
"Too many moves, your dance is a fright!"
The thorns laugh loud, "What a sight, what a sight!"
As laughter echoes into the night.

A fox takes stage, with a diabolical plan,
To make a new club, "The Glade's Best Clan!"
With moss as their rug, and leaves as a fan,
They giggle and wiggle, the fun never ran.

As dawn creeps in, with a yawning warm ray,
The fairies and critters pack up and play.
But in every rustle, you'll hear them say,
"See you tomorrow for more of this fray!"

Journey through Green Realms

In a forest thick with glee,
Leaves wiggle like they're free.
Squirrels joke on branches high,
Chasing shadows 'neath the sky.

Mossy paths and muddy shoes,
Nature laughs, it's never bruised.
In this realm, it's not so grand,
But oh, the fun at hand!

Breezes play and tickle trees,
Dancing lightly, setting ease.
Each step more silly than the last,
In this green world, troubles pass.

Laughter bubbles, wild and loud,
A wacky dance, we draw a crowd.
With every twist, a giggle shared,
In these realms, no one is scared.

The Tangle of Treads

Through twisting vines, we skid and glide,
Caught in laughter, what a ride!
Bumbling beetles lead the way,
In a game of run and play.

Over roots, we leap and bound,
Every stumble, joy unbound.
Shiny bugs in a silly race,
Each step takes us to a new place.

Together bound in silly fun,
Breathless laughs, we all outrun.
What a tangle, what a mess,
In this forest, pure excess!

With every trip, we find delight,
In a whirlwind of green and light.
So here's to every wild mishap,
In tangled woods, we'll take a nap!

Delicate Veins of Wonder

Under leaves, a secret path,
Mischief lies and playful wrath.
Tiny critters sing their song,
In this wonderland, we belong.

With whispers soft, they nudge and tease,
A game of hide and seek with ease.
Stems like arches, bent just so,
We tumble through with giggles low.

Petals flutter, soft as cake,
A merry chase we undertake.
Around the bend, we find a clown,
In this world, we just can't frown.

Mischievous sprites with winks and grins,
Make sure this fun never thins.
Delicate threads in laughter we weave,
In this green realm, we just believe!

Sprite's Sunlit Rest

Sunbeams dance on mossy beds,
Where giggling sprites lift their heads.
With tiny hats and bushy tails,
They tell tall tales of wander trails.

A picnic spread with acorn pies,
And berry juice for silly highs.
Bubbles rise from toadstool caps,
In this nook, we plot and map.

Around us swirls the dance of light,
As crickets chirp, we feel so bright.
A silly place to rest and play,
In this glade, we'll stay all day.

With laughter bold and grins so wide,
We frolic on this sunlit ride.
In this joyful, vibrant nest,
Life's a circus—so let's rest!

Verdant Whispers

In a patch of leafy hair,
A squirrel lost his nuts, oh dear!
He searched with flair, a comedy,
While birds above just laughed with glee.

The mossy carpet held a prank,
A snail slid by, its shell quite blank.
It thought it chic to take a stroll,
But face-planted in a muddy hole!

The crickets chirped their nightly tunes,
While frogs croaked jokes beneath the moons.
A toad in shades tried to look sleek,
But tripped and fell, oh what a geek!

The leaves all giggled in the breeze,
Humor drifts like fluff in trees.
In nature's realm, absurd is rife,
A hidden world of silly life.

Echoes in the Thicket

A raccoon wearing shiny threads,
Raided the pantry, made his beds.
He danced around with all his loot,
While bees buzzed on, refusing to toot!

The owls hooted jokes so loud,
They gathered in a raucous crowd.
A wise old sage piped up with zest,
'This party's better than all the rest!'

A rabbit with a top hat grand,
Pulled carrots from a magic hand.
The forest roared, they knew the trick,
As hungry foxes eyed him quick!

Down by the brook where giggles flowed,
Each pebble sang with tales bestowed.
Laughter echoed through the night,
In thickets where all jokes felt right.

Secrets of the Canopy

High above where the squirrels play,
A parrot told a joke that day.
It flapped its wings, with laughter sparked,
While acorns dropped and the laughter larked.

A sloth joined in, so very slow,
He laughed so hard, down he would go!
With arms spread wide, he'd miss the branch,
And tumble down in a leafy dance!

The sunbeams joined in, bright and bold,
Tickling leaves with stories untold.
Giggling vines in a tangled nest,
Wove tales of fun that never rest.

Beneath the leaves, a jester's game,
Each little critter sought their fame.
In secrets high, where humor thrives,
They craft their joy, it truly jives.

Dance of the Leafy Sprites

At dusk when shadows start to prance,
The sprites emerge for their wild dance.
They twirl and swirl with merry cheer,
Tickling branches, drawing near.

A gnome with boots too big to wear,
Joined in the fun, without a care.
He tripped on roots, went for a slide,
While mushrooms giggled, he took it in stride!

The fireflies lit up the scene,
Winking light like a teenage dream.
The ferns all waved in rhythm true,
Whispering jokes in shades of dew.

With laughter ringing through the glade,
Nature's giggles were well displayed.
In this wild, whimsical ballet,
Every creature danced, come what may!

Botanical Reveries

In the garden, plants start to dance,
Waving leaves in a playful prance.
Giggling petals, oh what a sight,
Whispering secrets in the moonlight.

Silly stems wear hats made of dust,
While roots play tag, oh what a must!
Flirting flowers blush with delight,
As bees trip over in sweet flight.

Cacti joke with spiky remarks,
While daisies organize fun parks.
Even the weeds want in on the fun,
They throw a party till the day is done.

When the sun yawns, they share a laugh,
Chasing shadows, a whimsical path.
Nature's humor, wild and free,
In this garden, joy's the decree.

The Enchanted Glade

In the glade where the wild things peek,
Squirrels giggle, and branches squeak.
Laughter bounces on the breeze,
As butterflies put on shows, if you please!

Mushrooms wear coats of polka dots,
While rabbits plot silly little spots.
Owls in glasses, wise and spry,
Critique the clouds drifting by.

The brook babbles jokes, so absurd,
While frogs croak lines that are quite word.
Mossy carpets invite a slide,
As crickets chirp, their hearts open wide.

In twilight's glow, a mischief unfolds,
Dancing fireflies break the molds.
The enchanted glade, oh what a spree,
A realm of laughter, truly carefree.

Shadows of the Green Dream

In shades of emerald, dreams take flight,
Whimsical shadows come alive at night.
The ferns in corners hold secrets tight,
As owls and raccoons get ready for a fright.

Giggling geckos race up the trees,
As snails on scooters drift with ease.
A talking stump shares ancient tales,
While mischievous squirrels plot their scales.

One sprout wears shoes far too big,
And hops around like a dancing pig.
Gusts of laughter in rustling leaves,
Echo through glens cloaked in webs of weaves.

When the moon peeks through, the fun ignites,
Chasing shadows, silly delights.
In the green dream, revelry reigns,
Nature's comedians, breaking all chains.

Nature's Lush Serenade

Beneath the canopy, laughter flows,
Where sunshine tickles, and mystery grows.
A chorus of critters with tunes to share,
Composing a symphony beyond compare.

Dancing dandelions sway to the beat,
While ants form a line, thinking they're neat.
Sunflowers twist for a better view,
As chatty chipmunks hold a review.

With ivy and vines weaving a spree,
Nature's stage set, come watch with glee.
The merry bug band performs with zest,
In this lush haven, smiles all the best.

When twilight descends, laughter prevailing,
In shadows and blooms, joy never failing.
Nature's serenade, sweet and bizarre,
Every leaf and petal shines like a star.

www.ingramcontent.com/pod-product-compliance
Lightning Source LLC
Chambersburg PA
CBHW071126130526
44590CB00056B/2493